THEMATIC UNIT
Numbers

Written by Jennifer Overend Prior, M. Ed.

Teacher Created Materials, Inc.
6421 Industry Way
Westminster, CA 92683
www.teachercreated.com
©2000 Teacher Created Materials, Inc.
Made in U.S.A.

ISBN-1-57690-617-5

Illustrated by
Ken Tunell

Edited by
Janet A. Hale, M.S. Ed.

Cover Art by
Denice Adorno

Table of Contents

Introduction

Numbers contains a captivating thematic unit. Its 80 exciting pages are filled with a wide variety of lesson ideas and activities designed for use with children at the early childhood level. For each of the four featured books, activities are included which set the stage for reading, encourage the enjoyment of the book, and extend the concepts gained. In addition, the theme is connected to the curriculum with activities in language arts (including language experience and writing suggestions), math, science, social studies, art, music, and life skills. Many of these activities encourage cooperative learning. Suggestions and patterns for bulletin boards are additional timesavers for the busy teacher. Furthermore, directions for child-created big books and culminating activities are included that allow children to synthesize their knowledge.

This thematic unit includes:

❑ **literature selections**—summaries of four children's books with related lessons (complete with reproducible pages) that cross the curriculum

❑ **language experience and writing ideas**—suggestions as well as activities that extend across the curriculum, including a big book

❑ **bulletin-board ideas**—suggestions for child-created and/or interactive bulletin boards

❑ **curriculum connections**—in language arts, math, science, social studies, art, music, and life skills

❑ **group projects**—to foster cooperative learning

❑ **culminating activities**—that require children to synthesize their learning to produce a product or engage in an activity that can be shared with others

❑ **a bibliography**—suggesting additional literature and nonfiction materials

---

To keep this valuable resource intact so it can be used year after year, you may wish to punch holes in the pages and store them in a three-ring binder.

Introduction (cont.)

Why Balanced Approach?

The strength of a balanced language approach is that it involves children in using all modes of communication—reading, writing, listening, illustrating, and doing. Communication skills are interconnected and integrated into lessons that emphasize the whole of language. Implicit in this approach is our knowledge that every whole—including individual words—is composed of parts, and directed study of those parts can help a child to master the whole. Experience and research tell us that regular attention to phonics, other word attack skills, spelling, etc., develops reading mastery, thereby fulfilling the unity of the whole language experience. The child is thus led to read, write, spell, speak, and listen confidently in response to a literature experience introduced by the teacher. In these ways, language skills rapidly increase, stimulated by direct practice, involvement, and interest in the topic.

Why Thematic Planning?

One very useful tool for implementing an integrated whole language program is thematic planning. By choosing a theme with a correlating literature selection for a unit of study, a teacher can plan activities throughout the day that lead to a cohesive, in-depth study of the topic. Children will be practicing and applying their skills in meaningful context. Consequently, they tend to learn and retain more. Both teachers and children will be freed from a day that is broken into unrelated segments of isolated drill and practice.

Why Cooperative Learning?

Besides academic skills and content, children need to learn social skills. No longer can this area of development be taken for granted. Children must learn to work cooperatively in groups in order to function well in modern society. Group activities should be a regular part of school life and teachers should consciously include social objectives as well as academic objectives in their planning. For example, a group working together to write a report may need to select a leader. The teacher should make this clear to the children and monitor the qualities of good leader-follower group interaction just as he/she would state and monitor the academic goals of the project.

Why Big Books?

An excellent cooperative, whole language activity is the production of big books. Groups of children, or the entire class, can apply their language skills, content knowledge, and creativity to produce a big book that becomes a part of the classroom library to be read and reread. These books make excellent culminating projects for sharing beyond the classroom with parents, librarians, other classes, etc.

Why Journals?

Each day your children should have the opportunity to write in a journal. They may respond to a book or an event in history, write about a personal experience, or answer a general "question of the day" posed by the teacher. The cumulative journal provides an excellent means of documenting writing progress.

Ten Black Dots

by Donald Crews

Summary

The bold colors and illustrations enhance the visual nature of this book—and you can count on that! Ten Black Dots uses dots to represent one sun, two fox eyes, and many more familiar objects. Counting all the way to ten, the rhyming text will have your children reading right along with you.

Sample Plan

Lesson 1

- Allow your children to explore the One, Two, Three bulletin-board display (page 6, Setting the Stage, #1).
- Count objects in the classroom (page 6, Setting the Stage, #2).
- Discuss the numbers of siblings and pets that the children have (page 6, Setting the Stage, #3).
- Read *Ten Black Dots* (page 6, Enjoying the Book, #1).
- Sing a number song (page 7, #4).

Lesson 2

- Re-read *Ten Black Dots*.
- Make a dots chart (page 6, Enjoying the Book, #2).
- Make dots booklets (page 6, Enjoying the Book, #3).
- Create a dots chart (page 6, Enjoying the Book, #4).

Lesson 3

- Practice counting the number of dots on dice and dominoes (page 7, #2).
- Make dotted number patterns (page 7, #2).
- Read a number poem (page 7, #1).

Lesson 4

- Discuss the numbers of eyes, ears, etc., on a variety of "faces" by completing How Many Do I Have? (page 7, #3).
- Have the children memorize the number poem introduced in Lesson 3 above.
- Make Black Dot Balloons (page 60).

Lesson 5

- Sing another number song (page 63).
- Make up hand movements to accompany your chosen number song.

Overview of Activities

Setting the Stage

1. Prepare your classroom by creating the bulletin-board display: "One, Two, Three!" (page 70). Have your children look for each displayed set of objects and share their discoveries.

2. Ask the class to count a variety of objects in the room, such as pencils, crayons, tables, toys, chalkboards, erasers, and glue bottles. Have the children place the displayed objects in like-item groups and then have them place each like-item group into smaller sets of two or three. Practice counting the number sets.

3. Ask the children to share how many siblings they have. Have those with zero siblings stand in one area of the room. The children with one sibling stand in an area adjacent to the "zero siblings" group. Continue this process until all of your children have been placed in your "human graph." Then, to transfer this visual display to a simple bar graph, provide each child with a piece of colored 3" x 3" (8 cm x 8 cm) paper. (Note: Each sibling group should be given a different color.) Have each child write his or her name on the provided paper and display the squares on a piece of chart paper that has been labeled with the numbers 0 to the greatest number of siblings represented in your class. For an extension, have the children do the same activity using "number of pets owned."

Enjoying the Book

1. Read *Ten Black Dots* and ask the children to count the number of dots on each page. Draw their attention to the fact that the dots in each illustration are being used to represent something else, such as the eyes on a fox or money in a piggy bank.

2. At the end of *Ten Black Dots,* the children will see charts on two pages that show a corresponding number of dots for each number. Your children can make the same kind of chart by making a counting-dots sheet. Provide each child with a black crayon, marker or pencil, and a piece of writing paper. Using a sheet of chart paper to demonstrate, write the number "0" and ask the children to do likewise on their writing paper. Then ask if any dots should be made. (No.) Then make a number "1" on the chart paper; have the children do the same on their paper. Again inquire on the need for dots. Make one round, black dot on the chart paper next to the number 1; have them do so as well. Repeat this process until you have the number "10" plus 10 black dots. Encourage the children to look at their dots sheets for counting activities.

3. To continue on with the theme in *Ten Black Dots,* have each child make his or her own Dots Booklet. Duplicate pages 8 through 12 for each child. Assemble each booklet by cutting apart the mini-pages on the dotted lines. Stack them in order, with the title page on top; staple the booklets together along the left side edge. Read each page to the children and have them use a black crayon to add the appropriate number of dots to match each illustration. When all of the dots have been added, have the children color the illustrations.

4. Read *Ten Black Dots* again and ask the children to identify the shape of a dot. Invite them to look for things around the room that are circle-shaped, such as balls, marbles, coins, the opening of a can, or the end of a pencil eraser. Draw their discoveries on chart paper and label it "Circles in Our Room." Then count the number of each item found, and write the total number next to each item; display the completed circles chart.

Fish Eyes: A Book You Can Count On

By Lois Ehlert

Summary

Counting and adding is colorfully entertaining with this engaging book. As your children pretend to be a counting fish, they will be guided past brightly colored fish in groups from one to ten. More fun is added by a recurring green fish that loves to comment on each fishy scene and encourages the reader to predict what the next page's number will be, based on the number of fish on the current page "plus one fish."

Sample Plan

Lesson 1

- Have your children count the fish on the prepared bulletin-board display (page 14, Setting the Stage, #1).

- Discuss ocean animals (page 14, Setting the Stage, #2).

- Read *Fish Eyes: A Book You Can Count On* (page 14, Enjoying the Book, #1).

- Count fish on an ocean storyboard (page 14, Enjoying the Book, #2).

- Introduce and sing the Number Songs (page 63).

Lesson 2

- Reread the book. Add a challenge to counting the book's fish (page 14, Enjoying the Book, #3).

- Sort objects in your mini-ocean (page 15, Extending the Book, #1).

- Make Fishy Eye Glasses (pages 21 and 22).

Lesson 3

- Make a fish graph (page 15, Extending the Book, #3).

- Identify number words (page 15, Extending the Book, #4).

- Color fish in a fishbowl (page 20).

- Create fish-cracker aquariums by gluing cheese fish-shaped crackers onto blue construction paper; display.

Lesson 4

- Sing Number Songs (page 63).

- Practice a few more simple addition problems (page 15, Extending the Book, #4).

- Count fish again using the ocean storyboard.

- Participate in the Dancing Fish activity (page 58).

Lesson 5

- Recite number poems (page 43)

- Read the book a final time.

- Complete How Many Do I Have? (page 57).

- Make Neon Fish (page 61).

Overview of Activities

Setting the Stage

1. Set the stage for a fishy numbers theme by creating the bulletin-board display: How Many Fishies in the Deep Blue Sea? (page 70).

2. Before reading *Fish Eyes: A Book You Can Count On*, ask your children to name all the animals they can think of that live in the ocean. List their responses on chart paper. As you read the story, see if their suggestions were/were not illustrated or mentioned in the book.

3. Show your children the cover of *Fish Eyes: A Book You Can Count On*. Ask your children to count the number of eyes they see in the fish. Based on the cover, ask them if a fish has more than one eye? Where's the other eye? (They may need help in understanding this rather abstract concept. You may want to make a paper fish with the eyes drawn in such a way that there is one eye on each side and demonstrate the cut out fish's similarities to the fish they will see in the book.) Looking at the fish collectively, have them count the number of mouths, fins, tails, and spots they see.

Enjoying the Book

1. Read the book to your children. Encourage them to identify the different colors of fish on each page. When the counting portion of the book begins, draw the children's attention to the little, dark-green fish that represents an addition problem before the page is turned. Pause briefly to allow the children to determine the answer. For example, "1 green fish plus me makes...2."

2. Continue the counting fun with a simple addition activity using an ocean story-board theme. Prepare the storyboard by covering a small, mobile bulletin board with blue felt; set aside. Onto tagboard, reproduce pages 17 to 19. Color, cut out, laminate, and back these pieces with sandpaper. Duplicate one set of pages 17-19 for each child; allow them to color and cut out the pieces. (Note: It is suggested that you provide each child with a self-sealing plastic bag in which to keep his or her pieces.) Provide each child, or every two children, with a large piece of blue construction paper. Then share some simple story problems for them to display by manipulating the patterns on the blue background. Use the felt background and sandpapered pieces to demonstrate the correct answers. Note: The number-word shells (page 18) can be used to demonstrate the language arts connection to the numbers utilized in the story problems. Here are a few story problem examples:

   - *There are two fish swimming. One more fish comes along. How many fish are in the ocean?*
   - *There are four fish in the ocean. How many fish tails do you see?*
   - *There is one fish in the ocean. How many eyes do you see? How many eyes does the fish have?*

3. For children who need a greater math challenge, turn to the first two-page spread in the book. This page shows a school of black, green, and yellow fish. Ask the children to count each school (set) of colored fish. (There are 14 black fish, 34 green fish, and two yellow fish.) You might even want to ask a related math question such as, "14 black fish plus two yellow fish equals how many fish?"

Overview of Activities *(cont.)*

Extending the Book

1. Your children will enjoy having a "mini-ocean" in the classroom. Put sand, rocks, and pebbles in the bottom of a plastic tub or baby pool. Fill the tub halfway with water. Add a variety of seashells as well as plastic fish water toys. Encourage your children to sort the shells, rocks, and fish in the "ocean" and count the number of objects in each group.

2. Set up a class aquarium. You can create one by simply using a fish bowl and a few goldfish. Encourage the children to find things on the fish that they can count, such as eyes, tails, fins, and mouths.

3. Enjoy a fishy graphing experience. Duplicate the Fishy Graph (page 16), one per child. Also provide each child with a small handful of assorted sea-animal crackers (goldfish, dolphins, and/or whales). Show the children how to graph their crackers by placing like crackers in columns on the graph. Have the children count the crackers in each column and discuss the results of their graphs. Challenge the children with questions such as, "Are there more dolphins or whales?" and "How many more goldfish than dolphins?"

4. Have your children practice simple addition using fish manipulatives. On small strips of paper, write simple addition equations. (Write the correct answer on the back of each paper strip.) Place the cards, along with a supply of goldfish crackers or fish candies, at a learning center. A child selects a card, uses the manipulatives to solve the problem, and then checks the answer on the back of the card. As a reward, allow the child to eat the manipulatives he or she has used.

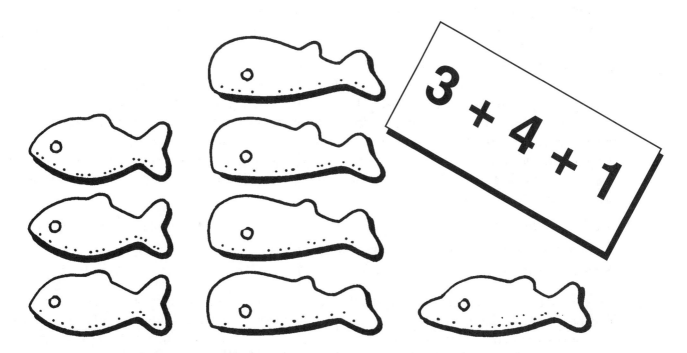

5. Try a fun movement activity by reading the poem Ten Little Fishies (page 43) as your children move to the words.

Fishy Graph

6	**5**	**4**	**3**	**2**	**1**

Ocean Story Patterns

Ocean Story Patterns *(cont.)*

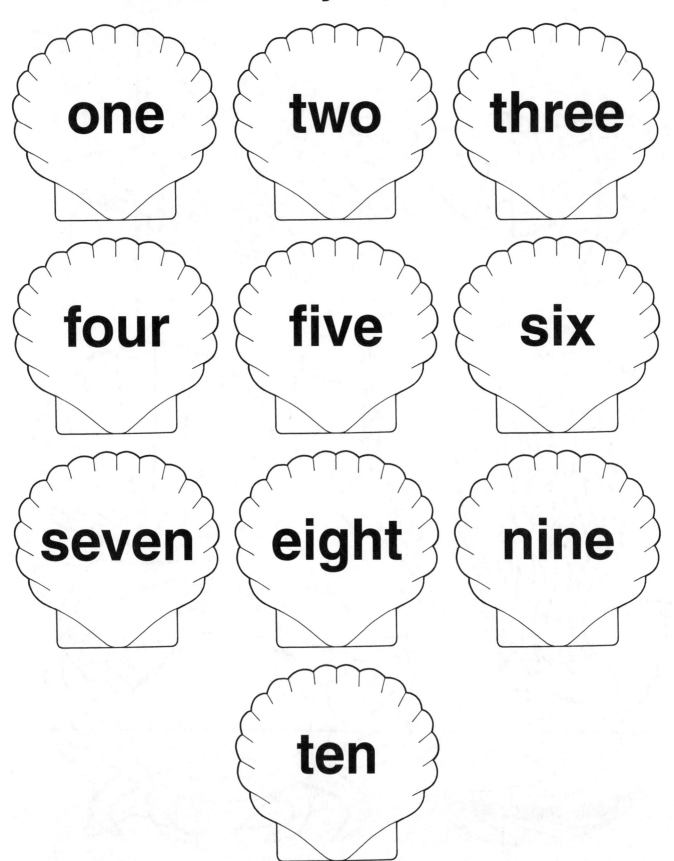

Ocean Story Patterns *(cont.)*

Fishbowl

Color 3 fish orange.

Color 4 fish red.

How many fish are colored? _____

How many fish are not colored? _____

How many fish in all? _____

Fishy Eyes

Materials

- glasses pattern (page 22)
- tagboard
- pencil
- scissors
- two 6" (15 cm) pipe cleaners
- crayons
- assorted colors of 9" x 12" (23 cm x 30 cm) construction paper
- glue

Directions

1. Prepare a pair of fishy eye glasses for each child by first tracing the pattern onto the tagboard and cutting it out.

2. Place the pattern atop a chosen color of construction paper. Trace around pattern with the pencil; cut out the glasses.

3. Punch holes in the sides of the glasses and attach pipe cleaners to create earpieces. Allow the child to color the glasses as desired. (Note: If desired, make decorations for the glasses by cutting interesting shapes from scrap construction paper pieces and gluing them onto the glasses.)

Uses

1. Have your children parade through the school to show off their fishy creations.

2. As you read the story, have the children wear their glasses and pretend they are fish.

3. Have your children wear their glasses as they act out simple fish story problems. (Example: Two fish were swimming. One more fish came along. How many fish were there?)

4. Recite the chant *Swim, Little Fishies*. Have your children wear their glasses as they act out the chant.

Swim, Little Fishies

Little fishies swim and
little fishies glide.
Little fishies jump and
little fishies dive
Swim, little fishies,
One, two, three, four.
Turn yourselves around and swim some more.

Fishy Eye Glasses

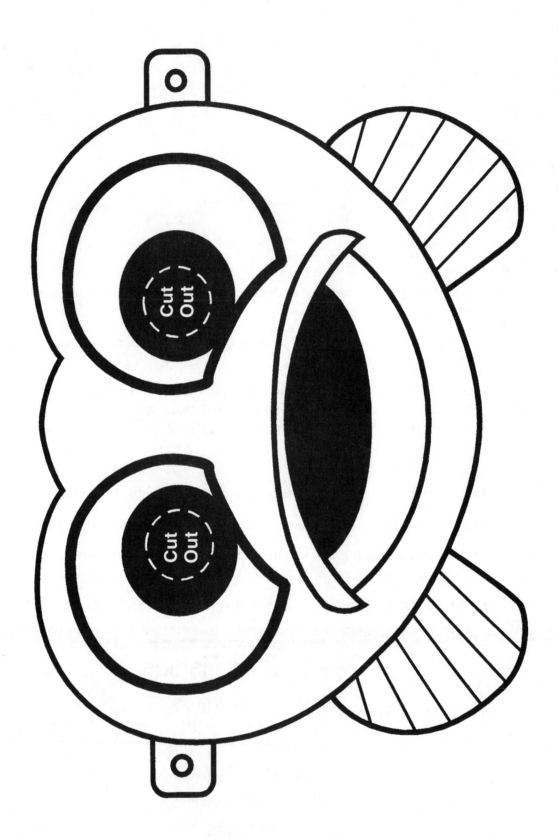

Anno's Counting Book

by Mitsumasa Anno

Summary

This wordless, picture book deals with the concept of one-to-one correspondence and the "power" of numbers. Each two-page spread features a different number using snowy illustrations. The fun of this book is enhanced by Anno's use of expounding numbers; so soon, even though the book begins with a snowy field of "none," there are more than enough wintry items to count!

Sample Plan

Lesson 1

- Take a walk to count outdoor objects (page 24, Setting the Stage, #1).
- Explore and discuss wordless books (page 24, Setting the Stage, #2.)
- Share *Anno's Counting Book* (page 24, Enjoying the Book, #1).
- Create a number scene (page 24, Enjoying the Book, #2).

Lesson 2

- Share *Anno's Counting Book* again (page 24, Enjoying the Book, #3).
- Make a number wheel (page 25, #1).
- Have the children learn their street addresses (page 25, #2).

Lesson 3

- Learn to write numbers using a writing number poem (page 25, #4).
- Sing a number song (page 63).
- Make a nature drawing (page 25, #5).

Lesson 4

- Make an art project (page 25, #6).
- Share *Anno's Counting Book* for a final time (page 25, #7).

Overview of Activities

Setting the Stage

1. Take your children on an outdoor walk to prepare for the reading of *Anno's Counting Book*. On your walk, ask the children to count the things they see—trees, buildings, birds, flowers, etc.

2. *Anno's Counting Book* has no words. Your children may have a difficult time understanding why a book has only pictures. Display an assortment of wordless books and show the children how pictures are used to tell the story.

Enjoying the Book

1. Share *Anno's Counting Book* with your children. For each page, say the number and then pause to allow the children time to carefully observe the illustrations. Continue in this manner throughout the entire book.

2. After viewing the book, your children can create their own number scene stories at a learning-center area. Begin by creating a simple background scene with sky and snow-covered hills, similar to the one on the zero page of *Anno's Counting Book*. Attach 25 squares of Velcro® to the snowy scene using a random placement (for example, in the sky and on the ground). Next, duplicate the mini-pictures on page 28. Color, cut out, and laminate the mini-pictures. Attach an opposite mate of Velcro to the back of each mini-picture. Reproduce the rebus cards (pages 29 and 30). Cut them out and laminate for durability.

To play, place the rebus cards facedown in five stacks according to their pictures (tree, house, bird, person, and flower). A child then selects and "reads" one rebus card from each stack. He or she then attaches the corresponding number of mini-pictures to the Velcro squares on the background display. Each time a child takes a turn a different scene will be created. (For example, a child may have chosen the rebus cards that represent: 2 flowers, 1 tree, 1 person, 4 birds, and 2 houses. The child would then find the needed number of corresponding mini-pictures and place them on the snowy background scene. Encourage the child to then tell a story about his or her number creation. When finished, he or she removes the mini-pictures and another child chooses one card from each stack and tells a new "number story."

3. Share *Anno's Counting Book* with your children again. This time, draw the children's attention to the counting strip on the left side of each illustration. (Note: On the zero page the strip is empty, but cubes will appear on the strip as the numbers increase.) Provide each child with a copy of page 31. Begin with one and have the children color in the corresponding number of squares on a strip as you re-look at each two-page spread.

Overview of Activities *(cont.)*

Extending the Book

1. Create a number wheel to help reinforce counting skills. Duplicate pages 26 and 27 for each child. Cut out both wheels and cut on the dotted lines of page 26 to make windows. Color the wheels, if desired. Stack the two wheels with the number wheel on the bottom. Attach them by pressing a brass fastener through the center dot. Then turn the wheel to reveal a number and set of flowers to count.

2. Memorizing a certain series of numbers, such as our phone number or address, is an important part of our everyday life. Impress upon your children the importance of knowing their street addresses by participating in the activity on page 59.

3. Play a game of one-to-one correspondence with your class. Place a set of one to nine crayons on a table. Have a child match the set by placing a corresponding number of crayons on the table. Continue in this manner with different number sets of crayons.

4. Duplicate copies of page 44, one per child. Practice writing numbers from zero to ten while reciting the number-writing poem on page 43. While reading the number poem, have the children trace the dotted lines to create the numbers. As they improve their number-writing skills, repeat the exercise by reading the poem and having them write the numbers independently without the use of dotted-line number patterns.

5. Your children can use their creativity while completing the nature-drawing activity on page 54. Duplicate copies for the children. Read the directions aloud as they draw and color the corresponding number of nature objects in the background.

6. The art project on page 62 results in a beautiful snowy-day picture, with an interesting touch. The salt mixture brushed atop the picture creates snowflake-like designs.

7. When reading *Anno's Counting Book* for the final time, allow individual children to discuss each number scene for his or her classmates. Encourage each child to talk about the featured number and how this number is represented in the illustration.

Number Wheel

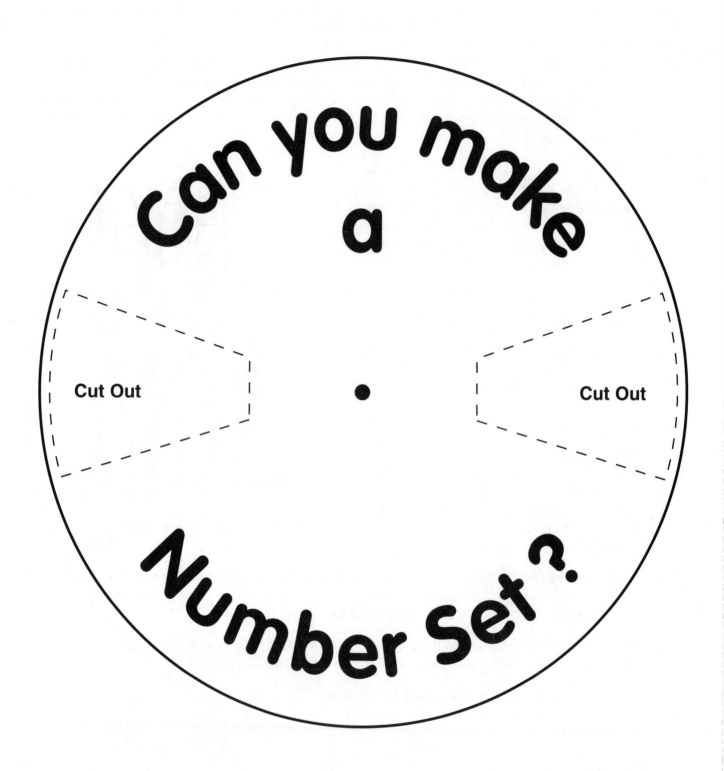

Number Wheel *(cont.)*

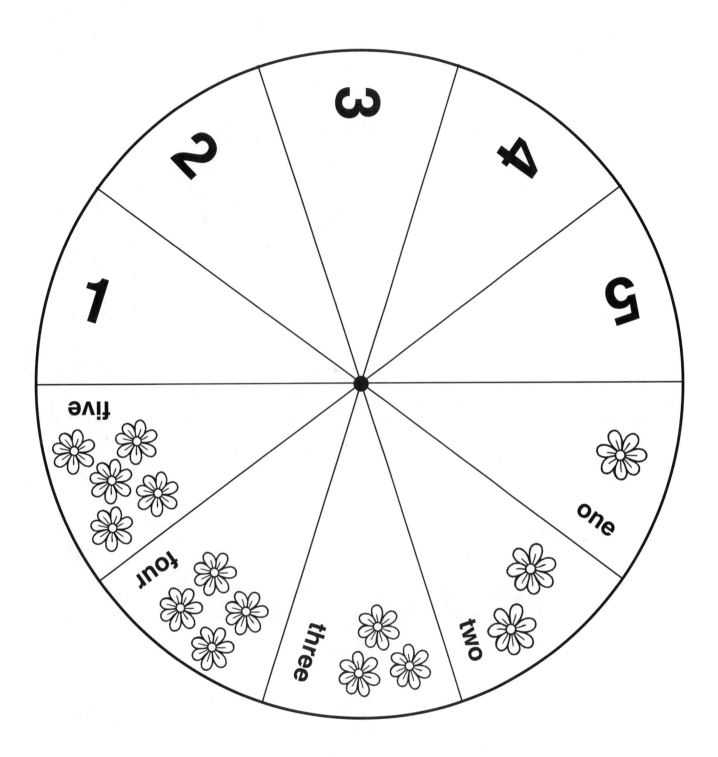

Storyboard Picture Patterns

Story Picture Rebus Cards

Story Picture Rebus Cards *(cont.)*

3 🐦 s	4 🐦 s	5 🐦 s
1 👦	2 👦 s	3 👧 s
4 👧 s	5 👦 s	1 🌼
2 🌼 s	3 🌼 s	4 🌼 s

Number Strips

| | | | | | | | | | | **10** |

| | | | | | | | | | | **9** |

| | | | | | | | | | | **8** |

| | | | | | | | | | | **7** |

| | | | | | | | | | | **6** |

| | | | | | | | | | | **5** |

| | | | | | | | | | | **4** |

| | | | | | | | | | | **3** |

| | | | | | | | | | | **2** |

| | | | | | | | | | | **1** |

Over in the Meadow

by Ezra Jack Keats

Summary

"Over in the meadow in the sand and the sun, lived an old mother turtle and her little turtle one." This age-old children's rhyme comes to life with the illustrations of Ezra Jack Keats. This up-beat counting book will have your children chanting or singing along as they count the animal babies from one to ten.

Sample Plan

Lesson 1

- Make a meadow mural (page 33, Setting the Stage, #1).
- Discuss meadow animals and their homes (page 33, Setting the Stage, #2).
- Look at animal books (page 33, Setting the Stage, #3).
- Read or sing *Over in the Meadow*.

Lesson 2

- Reread *Over in the Meadow*.
- Make meadow mini-books (page 33, Enjoying the Book, #2).
- Discuss the movements of animals (page 33, Enjoying the Book, #3).
- Assemble number puzzles (page 34, Extending the Book, #1).

Lesson 3

- Draw and number meadow animals (page 33, Enjoying the Book, #4).
- Make a big book (Page 34, Extending the Book, #3).

- Sing a number song (page 63).
- Complete Hiding in the Meadow (page 41).
- Make counting flipbooks (page 34, Extending the Book, #4).

Lesson 4

- Participate in a listening activity (page 33, Enjoying the Book, #4).
- Make a Bumblebee Counting Booklet (page 34, Extending the Book, #2).
- Read a number poem (page 43).
- Participate in a flannel-board activity (page 34, Extending the Book, #6).

Lesson 5

- Sing number songs (page 63).
- Count sets from 1–9 (page 34, Extending the Book, #7).
- Complete Meadow Matching (page 42).
- Make a meadow collage (page 62).
- Plan for a culminating picnic (page 69).

Overview of Activities

Setting the Stage

1. Have your children make a mural of a meadow. (Note: If they have never seen an actual meadow, try to show them some photographs or a video so that they have a concrete understanding of the concept.) Provide them with a large sheet of bulletin-board paper and encourage them to paint a background scene. Allow the background to dry. Using the animal patterns (copied from pages 73 and 74), have the children color, cut out, and glue them onto the background.

2. Prepare your children for the reading of *Over in the Meadow* by discussing animals that might be found in the meadow and around ponds. List their responses on chart paper and discuss the listed animals.

3. Display books with photographs of the animals featured in *Over in the Meadow*—turtles, foxes, robins, chipmunks, bees, beavers, frogs, owls, spiders, and rabbits. Encourage the children to closely observe the photographs, as well as share their experiences with animals and ask questions.

Enjoying the Book

1. Read or sing *Over in the Meadow*. Allow your children to talk about the animals they see in the book.

2. Your children can create their own counting mini-books. Duplicate pages 37–40, one per child. Cut the pages apart and stack them in sequence with the title page on top. Staple the pages together along the left-side edges. Each page has an illustration of a certain number of animals. Have each child count the animals and write the number on the line after the question. After responding to each question, have the child color the booklet pages.

3. Animals move in many different ways. Reread *Over in the Meadow* and ask the children to think about the ways that different kinds of animals move. How do turtles move? How do birds move? Encourage the children to pantomime the movements of the animals in the story.

   Continue the activity by having the children make the sounds that different animals make. If desired, have children make their own animal sounds booklet by coloring animal illustrations and writing simple patterned sentences next to each illustration, such as, "A bird chirps," or "A bee buzzes."

4. For the final reading of *Over in the Meadow*, have your children participate in a hands-on listening activity. Provide each child with copies of page 45–48. Allow them to color and cut out the animal pictures. As you read the story, have the children place the animal pictures in the proper numbered boxes (pages 47 and 48). At the end of the day, have the children take the number pages and animal cutouts home for additional practice.

Overview of Activities *(cont.)*

Extending the Book

1. Here's a fun way to continue practice counting. Duplicate pages 35 and 36 for each child. Assist children in cutting out the puzzle pieces, if necessary. Have each child color the pieces and then count the objects to match the corresponding pieces.

2. Making a Bumblebee Counting Booklet is another way to practice counting to ten. For each booklet, cut five 9" x 6¹/₂" (23 cm x 16.3 cm) construction-paper pages and staple them together along the left-side edge. Duplicate and cut apart one copy of page 50. Glue the cover page on the top construction-paper page; glue the sentence strips (one per page) in sequence at the bottom of the remaining pages. Read the text together. Have each child then create an illustration on each page.

3. Making a big book is a great way to teach children to work cooperatively. Follow the instructions on page 49 to create an animal counting book.

4. Flipbooks can be great counting fun! Prepare the flipbooks by duplicating page 55, one sheet per child. Cut out the two strips and stack. (The illustration strips should be on top.) Staple the strips together along the top edge; then carefully cut along the dotted lines. Have children color the illustrations. To use the booklets, the child counts the animals on a flip page and then flips it up to reveal the number below.

5. Here's another way to allow your children to practice their counting skills. Prepare for the activity by cutting out various animal pictures from magazines. Glue sets of like animals on large index cards. Print corresponding numbers on another set of cards. To play, the children match the correct number card to the correct animal picture card by looking at all of the cards, or playing in a memory-game fashion.

6. Make a counting flannel board of animal pictures. Reproduce the animal pictures (pages 73 and 74) on tagboard. Color the pictures with markers; cut out and glue small sandpaper pieces to the backs of the cards. The children can then place the cards on a flannel board and count them.

7. Group stuffed or plastic bunnies (or other meadow animals) in sets of ten. You may also want to use sets of classroom items, such as books or pencils. Have the children count each set of objects. Continue this process with sets from one to nine.

8. There are many other delightful number books that you can share with your children. See the Annotated Bibliography on pages 79 and 80 for suggestions.

Meadow Mini-book

Counting in the Meadow

Name _____

How many animals are in the meadow? _____

How many turtles dig? _____

Meadow Mini-book *(cont.*

How many foxes run? _____

How many birdies sing? _____

How many chipmunks play? _____

Meadow Mini-book *(cont.)*

How many honeybees hum? _____

How many beavers build? _____

How many polliwogs swim? _____

Meadow Mini-book *(cont.)*

How many owls wink? _____

How many spiders spin? _____

How many bunnies hop? _____

Hiding in the Meadow

Find and color the animals in the meadow.

Meadow Matching

Color, cut, and glue to complete the animals.

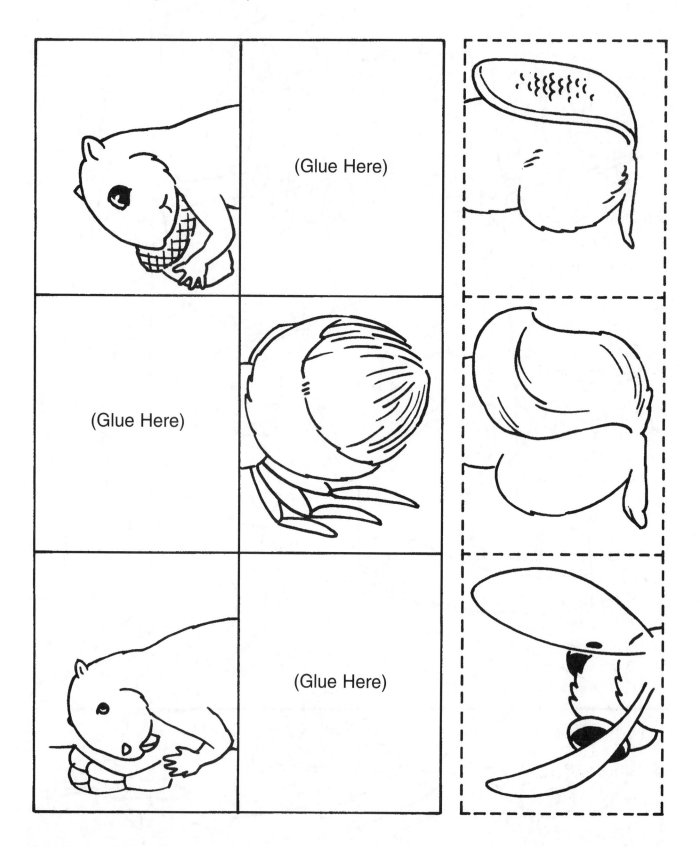

Poetry Counts

Counting to Ten

One, two, three, look at me.
I can count—as you can see.
One, two, three . . .
Four, five, six . . .
Seven, eight, nine, ten . . .
And that's the end!

Ten Little Fishies

Ten little fishies in the deep, blue sea,
The first one said, "Come play with me."
The second one said, "Let's swim in a line."
The third one said, "The water's fine!"
The fourth one said, "Let's dive down deep."
The fifth one said, "I think I'll sleep."
The sixth one said, "Let's leap in the air."
The seventh one said, "Oh, I don't dare!"
The eighth one said, "We are cool."
The ninth and tenth ones said, "Together we make a school!"
Ten little fishies in the deep blue sea,
I wish you could play with me!

Writing Numbers

0 Around the track, just once you go—that is how you make a zero.
1 Top to bottom, now you are done—that is how you make a one.
2 Around and back on the railroad track—two, two, two.
3 Around the tree, around the tree—that is how you make a three.
4 Down and over, and down once more—that is how you make a four.
5 First go down and give me a tummy, add on a hat—a five sure looks funny.
6 Down you go and add a loop—six rolls 'round like a Hula Hoop®.
7 Across the sky and down from heaven—that is how you make a seven.
8 Make an S, but do not wait, come back up to make an eight.
9 First a loop and then a line—that is how you make a nine.
10 Make a one and add a zero. You've made a ten and you're a hero!

Numbers Count

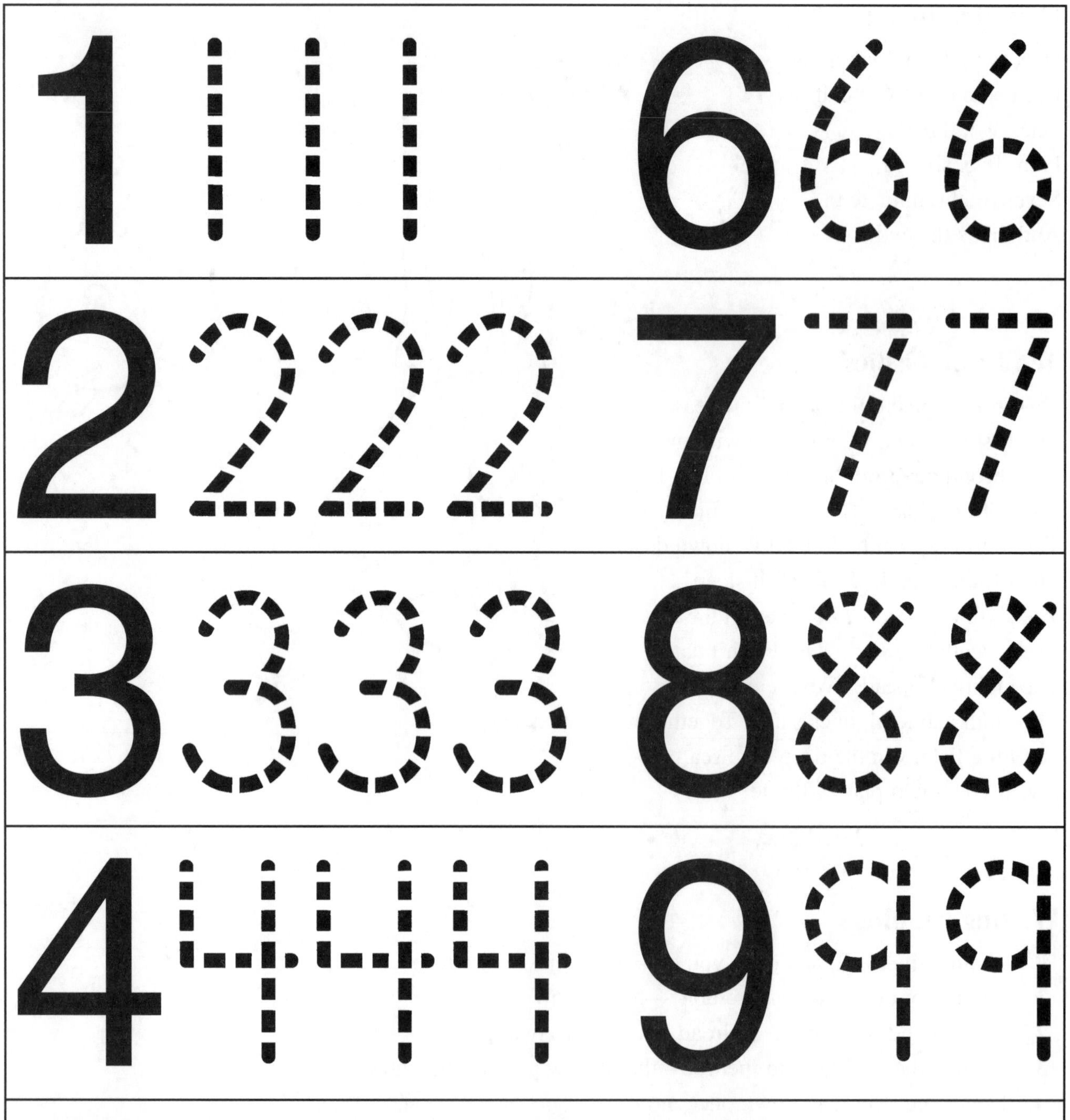

1 | | | | | 6 6 6

2 2 2 2   7 7 7

3 3 3 3   8 8 8

4 4 4 4 4   9 9 9

5 5 5 5   10 10

Counting Meadow Animals

Color the pictures and cut out the boxes.

Counting Meadow Animals (cont.)

Color the pictures and cut out the boxes.

46

Counting Meadow Animals *(cont.)*

As your teacher reads the story, place the animal in the correct number places.

```
┌──────────────────────────┐   ┌──────────────────────────┐
│                          │   │                          │
│                          │   │                          │
│                          │   │                          │
│                        1 │   │                        2 │
└──────────────────────────┘   └──────────────────────────┘

┌──────────────────────────┐   ┌──────────────────────────┐
│                          │   │                          │
│                          │   │                          │
│                          │   │                          │
│                        3 │   │                        4 │
└──────────────────────────┘   └──────────────────────────┘

        ┌──────────────────────────┐
        │                          │
        │                          │
        │                          │
        │                        5 │
        └──────────────────────────┘
```

Counting Meadow Animals *(cont.)*

As your teacher reads the story, place the animal in the correct number places.

Making a Big Book

Big books provide wonderful, language-arts experiences that combine reading, writing, speaking, and listening. This big-book idea also encourages artistic creativity and counting skills.

Steps

1. Before making the big book, share a counting book, such as *Count!* by Denise Fleming (Henry Holt, 1995). Discuss the different types and number sets of animals on each page. Draw your children's attention to the actions of each animal.

2. Display a large sheet of paper (at least 12" x 18"/30 cm x 46 cm).

3. Begin by writing the number 1 on the paper. Have a child name an animal and its action. For example, "1 rabbit hops." Write their provided statements near the bottom of the pages.

4. Continue in this manner with remaining nine pages, each labeled with a number two through ten. Encourage the children to name the animals and their actions for each of the number pages. For example, "2 birds fly," or "3 zebras run."

5. Give a page to each pair of children to illustrate.

6. Stack the completed pages in correct sequence and add a title page. Align the edges and staple the pages together along the left edge to create the book's spine.

Extensions

*   Encourage the children to read the book to one another.

*   Have the children share the book with visitors during the culminating activity.

*   Invite children from other classes to visit for a reading of the book.

*   Display the book in your library for all to see.

Bumblebee Counting Booklet

Ten Little Bumblebees

by _____

One, two, three, buzzing little bumblebees.

Four, five, six, buzzing in the trees.

Seven, eight, nine, buzzing in a row.

Ten little bumblebees, buzzing as they go!

50

Ocean Addition

2 + 1 = __

 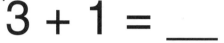

3 + 1 = __

3 + 2 = __

4 + 4 = __

5 + 1 = __

4 + 2 = __

3 + 3 = __

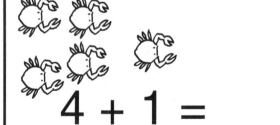

4 + 1 = __

5 + 2 = __

4 + 3 = __

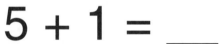 

Nature Drawings

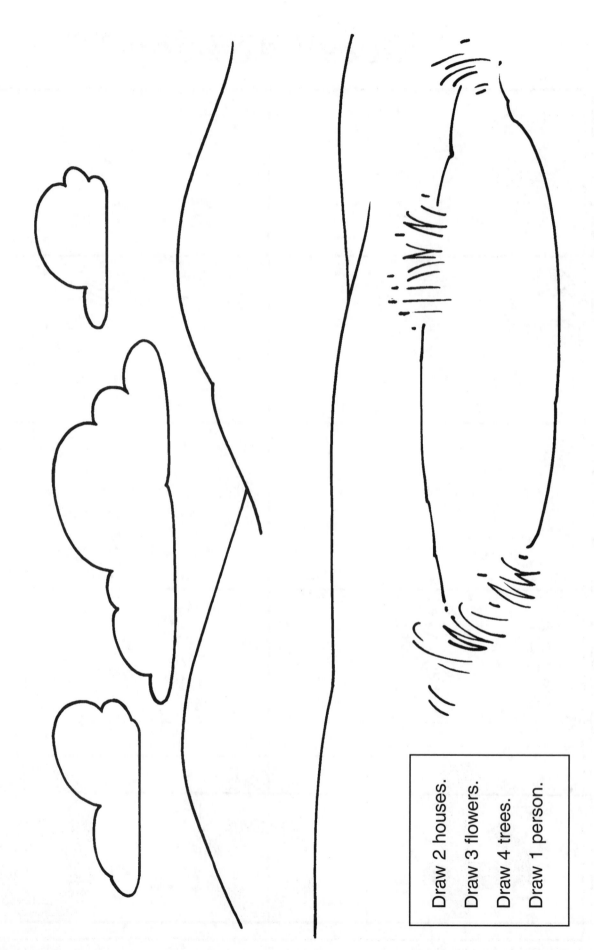

Draw 2 houses.

Draw 3 flowers.

Draw 4 trees.

Draw 1 person.

Flip Counting Books

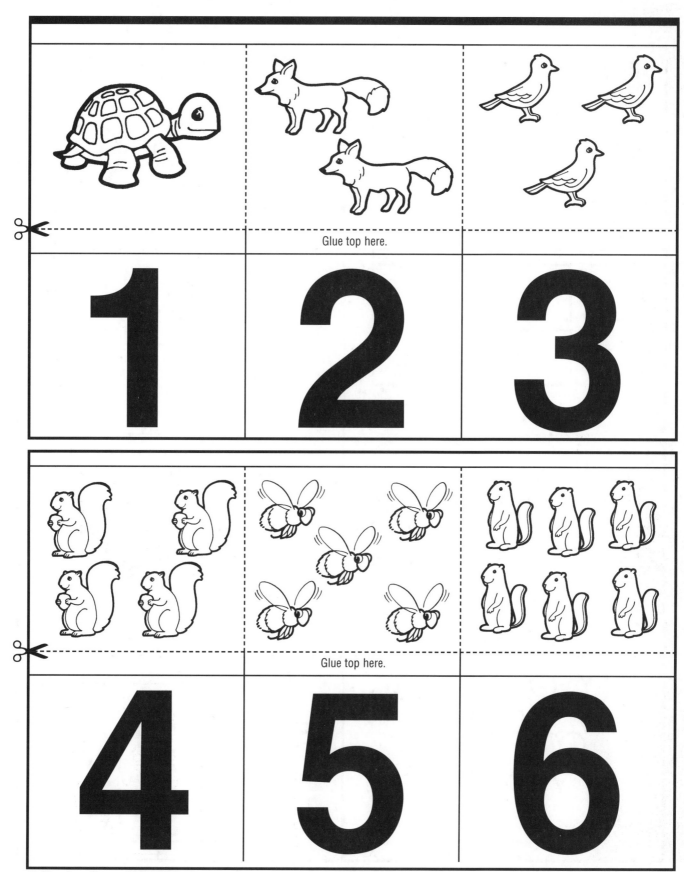

Glue top here.

Glue top here.

Counting Sets

How many?

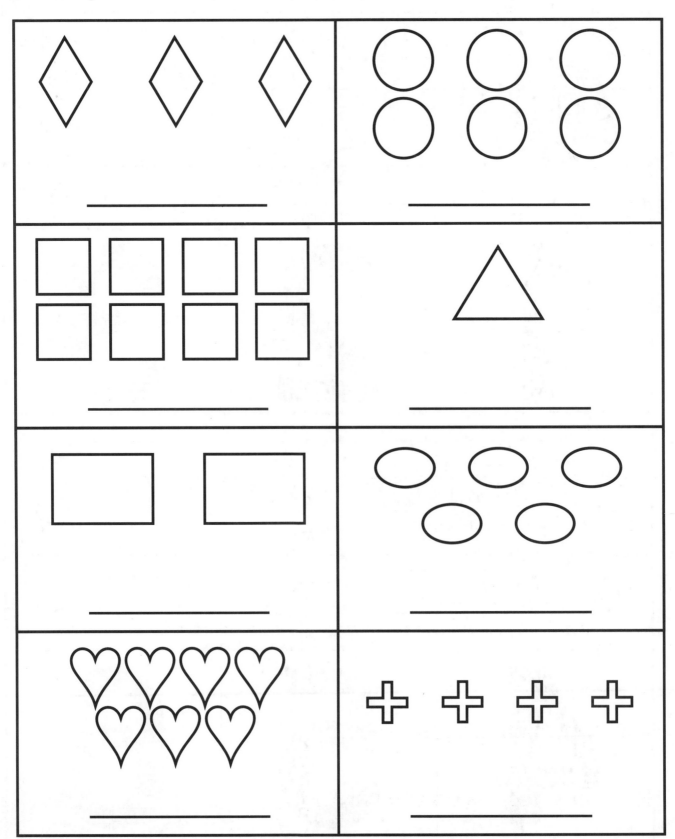

56

How Many Do I Have?

I have _____ 👁👁 .

I have _____ 👄 .

I have _____ ✋ on one hand.

I have _____ 🖐🖐 on two hands.

I have _____ 👣 .

I have _____ .

I have _____ 👃 .

I have _____ .

Challenge:

How many teeth do you have? _____

How many freckles do you have? _____

Dancing Fish

Try this simple experiment and your children will watch in amazement as the fish dance to the top of the container.

Materials

- large, glass container
- water
- vinegar
- raisins
- baking soda

Directions

1. Fill a glass container with water. Mix in $1/3$ cup (80 mL) of vinegar and 2 teaspoons (10 mL) of baking soda. Stir gently.

2. Add a few raisins (representing fish) to the container. They will sink to the bottom at first, but then they will rise to the surface. The "fish" will continue rising to the surface and sinking back to the bottom for several hours.

3. As small groups of children observe the dancing fish up close, ask them to identify the number of raisins (fish) at the top and bottom of the jar at different times. How many are resting on the bottom? How many are floating on top? How many are rising?

Why It Works

When the vinegar and baking soda are combined, they create a chemical reaction that produces carbon dioxide. The carbon dioxide bubbles collect on the raisins on the bottom of the jar. Since the bubbles are lighter than the water, they lift the raisins to the surface, where several of the bubbles escape into the air. The raisins once again sink to the bottom where they collect more bubbles and become buoyant once again.

My Address Is...

Teaching your children to memorize their street address is an important skill. It can be vital if they become lost or need to call 911 in an emergency.

Begin by duplicating the lower portion of this page for each child. Write each child's address on the lines and have him or her repeat it back to you. Then gather all of the children together in a circle, with address sheets in hand. Say, "Is there a 2 in your address?" The children check their address sheets and any child with the number 2 in the street address raises his or her hand. In turn, have those children recite their addresses. For example, "My street address is 4295 E. Desert Lane." When all appropriate children have recited their addresses, call out another number, continue until you have used all the numbers zero to nine. At the conclusion of this activity, present your children with an address award (page 76).

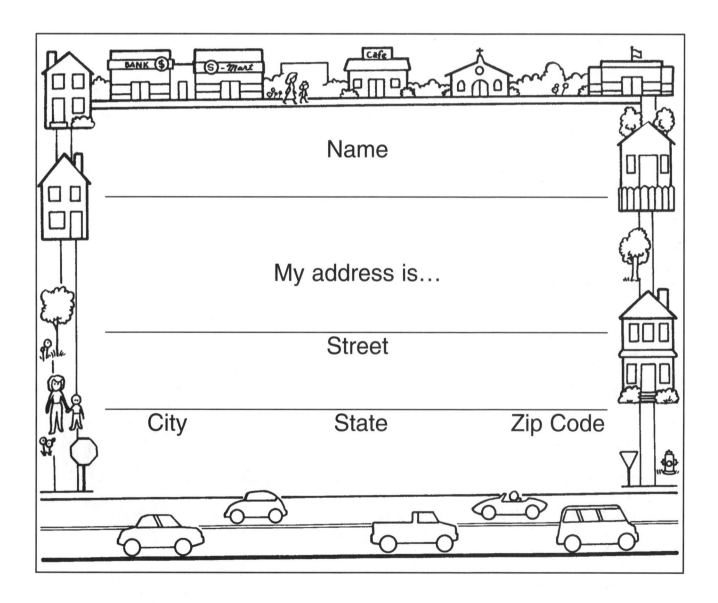

Name

My address is...

Street

City   State   Zip Code

One Black Dot Balloon

Materials

- balloon pattern (page 71)
- black construction paper
- scissors
- glue
- 13" x 18" (33 cm x 46 cm) sheet of light-blue construction paper
- 6-inch (15.2 cm) length of yarn or string
- assorted colors of construction paper
- silver glitter (optional)

Directions

1. Duplicate two copies of the balloon patterns (page 71). Cut them out to be used as tracers: one balloon-shaped tracer and then the four separate shapes.

2. Trace the balloon pattern onto the black construction paper; cut out the shape. Glue the balloon to the light-blue construction paper.

3. Squeeze a six-inch (15 cm) vertical trail of glue extending below the balloon. Attach the yarn or string to the glue trail.

4. Trace the shapes onto assorted colors of construction paper and cut them out. Glue them onto the balloon as decorations. (Optional: Add dots or lines of silver glitter to the balloon for additional decorations.) Display on a bulletin board or wall space.

5. Teach your children this poem to recite as visitors view your balloon display.

Black dot, black dot on a string.
Oh, what happiness you bring.
Black dot, black dot in the air.
You are floating here and there.
Black dot, black dot, big balloon.
Fly away and touch the moon.

Neon Fish

Materials

- fish pattern (page 72)
- tagboard
- pencil
- scissors
- assorted neon-colored paper
- glue
- 13" x 18" (33 cm x 46 cm) sheet of black construction paper

Directions

1. Duplicate the desired fish pattern and trace it onto tagboard. Cut out the tagboard fish to be used as a tracer; discard the paper scraps.

2. Trace the fish onto a chosen color of neon paper; cut the fish out.

3. Glue the fish to the black construction-paper background sheet.

4. Using the assorted neon colors, cut out stripes, dots, and other decorations. Glue them onto the fish.

5. If desired, add seaweed and other background decorations to the black construction paper to complete the project.

Fishies in the Sea

Materials

- waxed paper (two sheets)
- newspaper
- crayon shavings
- construction-paper fish cutouts
- warm iron

Directions

1. Place one sheet of waxed paper atop several sheets of newspaper.

2. Sprinkle crayon shavings atop the waxed paper.

3. Place one or two fish cutouts on top of the shavings.

4. Place the remaining sheet of waxed paper on top of the first, aligning the edges.

5. Place another sheet of newspaper atop the project and press with a warm iron to melt the crayon shavings.

Snowy Day Picture

Materials

- one sheet of blue 9" x 13" (23 cm x 33 cm) construction paper
- white tempera paint
- paintbrush
- crayons or markers
- 2 teaspoons (10 mL) of salt
- 1 teaspoon (5 mL) of liquid starch
- water
- mixing cup
- mixing spoon

Directions

1. At the bottom of the blue sheet of construction paper, paint an area of snow using white tempera paint. Allow the paint to dry.

2. Using the crayons or markers, create an outdoor snow scene, including house, trees, birds, and people.

3. Give the illustration an icy look by brushing a prepared mixture of the salt, liquid starch, water, and a few drops of white tempera paint over the entire picture; allow to dry.

Meadow Collage

The artwork of Ezra Jack Keats is truly unique, including his use of collage in creating illustrations and backgrounds. Your children can make a meadow collage in the same unique style.

Materials

- one sheet of 9" x 13" (23 cm x 33 cm) dark-colored construction paper
- glue
- colored construction-paper scraps
- magazines
- crayons or markers

Directions

1. For the collage background, tear off small pieces from the construction-paper scraps. Glue the torn pieces onto the dark-colored construction paper in a random fashion.

2. For the foreground, tear small pieces of scenic magazine pictures and glue them onto the background; allow to dry.

3. Complete the picture by using crayons or markers to create trees, grass, and meadow animals.

Number Songs

I Can Count
(Sung to the tune of *Jimmy Cracked Corn*)

I can count,
1, 2, 3.
I can count,
4, 5, 6.
I can count,
7, 8, 9,
until I get to ten.

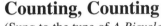

Counting, Counting
(Sung to the tune of *A Bicycle Built for Two*)

Counting, counting,
It is so fun to do.
I love counting,
Won't you count with me, too?
We start with the number one,
And count till we are done.
1, 2, 3,
4, 5, 6,
7, 8, 9, and ten!

The Number Song
(Sung to the tune of *The Muffin Man*)

Number one is all alone, all alone, all alone.
Number one is all alone, one, one, one.
Number two is me and you, me and you, me and you.
Number two is me and you, two, two, two.
Number three is next, you see, next, you see, next, you see.
Number three is next, you see, three, three, three.
Number four is just one more, just one more, just one more.
Number four is just one more, four, four, four.
Now we get to number five, number five, number five.
Now we get to number five, one—two, three—four, five.

Time for Counting
(Sung to the tune of *Allouette*)

Time for counting,
It is time for counting.
Time for counting,
You know what to do.
Starting out with number one. Just one finger—number one.
Number one, number one, oh…
Show two fingers one and two. We can count them one and two.
One and two, one and two, oh…
After two is number three. Show three fingers—one, two, three.
One—two—three, one—two—three, oh…
We can add on just one more. Then we'll get to number four.
One—two—three—four, one—two—-three—four, oh…
Now we are at number five. A full hand of fingers—five.
One—two—three—four—five, one—two—three—four—five!

Animal Songs

Since many of the stories used in this thematic unit pertain to animals, create verses to make class animal songs with this activity. Begin by brainstorming a list of different kinds of animals with your children. Record responses on chart paper. Then list an action (verb) for each animal. Decide where each animal lives. Then use the generated list to fill in the blanks. Sing your song to the tune of *Bingo*.

There was a _____ in the

_____,

and this is what it did.

_____, _____,

_____, _____, _____.

_____, _____,

_____, _____, _____.

_____, _____,

_____, _____, _____.

The _____ in the _____.

Example:

There was a rabbit in the woods
and this is what it did.
Hop, hop,
hop, hop, hop.
Hop, hop,
hop, hop, hop.
Hop, hop,
hop, hop, hop.
The rabbit in the woods!

64

Cooking Fun

Funny Face

Ingredients

- 1 large round cracker
- peanut butter
- 1 plastic knife
- 1 maraschino cherry half
- 2 chocolate chips
- 3 red licorice strings
- 4 raisins

Directions

1. Spread a layer of peanut butter on the cracker.
2. Place the facial features and hair on the peanut butter in sequential order: 1 cherry for the nose, 2 chocolate chips for the eyes, 3 licorice strings for the hair, and 4 raisins for the mouth.

Rabbit in the Woods

This edible treat is a nice addition to the *Over in the Meadow* story.

Ingredients

- 1 sturdy paper plate
- 1 leaf of lettuce
- 1 canned pear half
- 2 raisins
- 1 cinnamon candy
- 2 blanched almond slices
- 1 tablespoon (15 mL) cottage cheese

Directions

1. Place the lettuce leaf on the paper plate.
2. Place the pear half in the center of the lettuce leaf.
3. At the smaller end of the pear, create the rabbit's face by pressing in the cinnamon candy for a nose, the raisins for eyes, and the almond slices for ears.
4. At the opposite end of the pear, place a spoonful of cottage cheese for the tail.

Number Cookies

There are many commercially made sugar cookies in the shape of the numbers 0 through 9. If you cannot find them in your area, most kitchen-supply stores carry number cookie cutters. Using your favorite sugar cookie recipe, whip up a batch of edible counting fun!

Movement Chants

Recite the following chants as your children act out the words.

Swim, Little Fishies

Little fishies swim and
little fishies glide.
Little fishies jump and
little fishies dive
Swim, little fishies,
One, two, three, four.
Turn yourselves around and swim some more.

A Day in the Snow

Let's get ready for a day in the snow.
One, two, three, it's time to go.
Put on your coat and put on your hat.
Put on your gloves as easy as that.
Slide through the snow.
Throw snow in the air.
Let those snowflakes fall in your hair.
Burr! I'm cold. It's time to go.
What a great day we had playing in the snow!

Animal Show

It's time for the animal animal show.
Leap like a frog and go, go, go.
Buzz like a bumblebee, little owls hoot.
Run like a baby fox, cute, cute, cute.

It's time for the animal, animal show.
Crawl like a turtle and go, go, go.
Spin like a spider and sing like a bird,
prettiest song you've ever heard.

It's time for the animal, animal show.
Choose your favorite animal and go, go, go!

Web Sites You Can Count On!

Children's Storybooks Online

http://www.magickeys.com/books/

Access this Web site to find a long list of online storybooks. Simply click on the desired story and enjoy simple stories and delightful animation. This site includes a story entitled *The Counting Story*.

The Counting Game

http://home.earthlink.net/~cmalumphy/countinggame.html

This Web site has been designed for children to use. They count sets of colored shapes and click on the correct number. A rising thermometer tracks progress.

Funschool.com

http://www.funschool.com/

This site contains fun games and activities for children from Pre-K through Sixth Grade. For the young ones, you'll find activities for number matching, and for connecting and sequencing numbers.

Helping Your Child Learn Math—Math on the Go

http://www.ed.gov/pubs/parents/Math/resources.html

This parent-friendly Web site gives ideas for teaching children to identify numbers in the real world. Activities include, looking for numbers on buildings, phone numbers on business vehicles, and games relating to license-plate numbers.

Helping Your Child Learn Mathematics

http://www.pmct.org/math.html

This Web site shares simple activities that parents and teachers can use to foster math skills. Activities include the use of puzzles, cards, money, cooking activities, and much more.

Kayleigh's Playground

http://kayleigh.tierranet.com

At this site you can find a large selection of interactive learning activities for young children. There are online activities for learning letters, numbers, colors, and shapes, as well as music, games, and even online stories.

Web Sites You Can Count On! *(cont.)*

Kid's Domain Downloads

http://www.kidsdomain.com/down/index.html

This Web site is a virtual gold mine of downloadable software programs. Freeware, shareware, and demo programs are available for Macintosh or PC in a variety of subject areas.

Learning Partners—Let's do Math!

http://www.kidsource.com/kidsource/content/Learning_math.html

Here's another great Web site for parents. They'll find more ideas for identifying and using numbers in the real world.

Math Activities for Children and Families

http://www.eduplace.com/hmco/school/projects/mathp.html

Here's a great Web site for teachers and parents, including easy and fun math-related activities, such as making a fruit graph and matching money.

Math and the Myth of 1, 2, 3

http://www.kidsource.com/kidsource/content4/math.myth.html

This informative Web site gives parents and teachers ideas for providing real-life math experiences for children.

Math for Fun

http://www.alphalink.com.au/~alain/math/math.htm

By accessing this Web site, you can download a simple math game called Math for Fun. This simple math game is only available for Windows 3.1 and higher and teaches children basic operations, use of the keypad, and simple money transactions.

Mighty Math Club

http://www.mathclub.com

Teachers and parents will enjoy this site that is filled with interactive math games for online or offline learning experiences.

Summertime Funtime Activities

http://www.kidsource.com/kidsource/content2/summertime.fun.html

This Web site provides a list of summertime activities related to math, science, and reading. A simple activity for almost every day of summer makes this a great resource for parents.

It's Picnic Time!

For a culminating activity, plan a picnic using your favorite literature title featured in this thematic unit. Have a beach picnic to accompany *Fish Eyes: A Book You Can Count On*, have a snowy day picnic to accompany *Anno's Counting Book*, or have a meadow picnic to accompany *Over in the Meadow*.

Create the Atmosphere

1. Have the class create mural scenes of the ocean, the snowy outdoors, or the meadow to display around the room. Also display child-created items made throughout the *Numbers* unit.

2. Have the children record the number songs (page 63) onto a cassette tape and have the songs playing as guests arrive.

3. Plan the picnic menu by having children prepare foods from the Life Skills section (page 65) or serve fish crackers or Gummi® fish for an ocean theme; frozen treats for the snow-day picnic; and small sandwiches for the meadow picnic.

4. Duplicate, cut out, and color the number of guest awards needed (page 76).

5. Reproduce and distribute the invitation (page 75) to your invited guests.

Picnic Activities

1. Spread beach towels or picnic blankets on the floor in a cleared area of the classroom.

2. Have the children recite number poems (page 43). They may want to create movements to accompany the recitings.

3. Display the class big book (page 49). Encourage the children to read the book to your guests.

4. Have the children teach the guests how to play a variety of number games and puzzles, such as Matching Numbers and Dots (page 7, Extending the Book, #2), Ocean Story Problems (page 14, Enjoying the Book, #2) or Number Puzzles (page 34, Extending the Book, #1).

5. Read the featured number book (that matches your theme) or select additional books to read from the Bibliography (pages 79 and 80).

6. Before leaving, provide each guest with a prepared award.

Bulletin-Board Ideas

One, Two, Three!

Create a bulletin-board display that includes a variety of pictured objects or animals. Display various sets of one, two, and three (objects/animals). Encourage your children to look for and count the various displayed sets.

How Many Fishies in the Deep Blue Sea?

To make this display, create a background of blue bulletin-board paper. Attach strips of green crepe paper for seaweed. Attach fish cutouts (page 72) in several different colors. Ask the children to count the fish. How many fish are there in all? How many red fish are there? How many yellow fish?

Balloon Shape Patterns

Fish Patterns

     72

Big Book Patterns

Big Book Patterns *(cont.)*

Invitation

It's Picnic Time!

We're having a picnic.

Place: _____

Date: _____

Time: _____

We're counting on you to join us!

It's Picnic Time!

We're having a picnic.

Place: _____

Date: _____

Time: _____

We're counting on you to join us!

Awards

1 2 3 4 5 🏠 6 7 8 9 0

I know my address—numbers and all!

8 7 6 5 4 3 2 1   1 2 3 4 5 6 7 8

Name: _____

Date: _____

1 2 3 4 5 🏠 6 7 8 9 0

You Count!

2 3

1

Thanks for joining us in

_____.

Name: _____

Date: _____

Annotated Software Bibliography

Arthur Math Carnival—ActiMaths Software
by Microsoft

Join Arthur at the carnival for a variety of math games. Children practice addition, subtraction, fractions, money concepts, and much more. Appropriate for ages 4–8. Available for Windows only.

Davidson's Learning Center Series: Kindergarten
by Davidson

This interactive software program helps to prepare young children for kindergarten. You'll find math skills for learning bigger/smaller, counting and quantities, time concepts, and problem solving. In addition to math skills, children learn letter and word recognition skills. Appropriate for ages 4–6. Available for Windows and Macintosh.

Disney's Ready for Math with Pooh
by Disney Interactive

With this interactive software program, children join Pooh and friends to practice counting, number forming, addition, and subtraction. Appropriate for ages 3–6. Available for Windows or Macintosh.

Easy Early Math
by Sierra On Line

Based on the NCTM standards, this program combines the use of math manipulatives and animated graphics to learn basic operations. Available for Windows only.

Fisher-Price Ready for PreSchool
by Knowledge Adventure

This three-level program takes place at a circus and focuses on a variety of preschool skills in the areas of math and language. Appropriate for ages 2–4. Available for Windows and Macintosh.

Interactive Math Journey
by The Learning Company

Children participate in 25 activities in search of the mathmagician. Skills include patterns, addition, subtraction, measurement, fractions, and multiplication.

James Discovers Math
by Broderbund

This delightfully animated program offers interactive practice with reasoning, problem solving, measurement, geometry, numeration, and computation. Appropriate for ages 5–9. Available for Windows or Macintosh.

JumpStart Learning Games Numbers
by Knowledge Adventure, Inc.

Young children will enjoy this arcade-style learning environment as they enhance skills in addition, subtraction, sequences, counting, and much more. Appropriate for ages 5–8. Available for Windows and Macintosh.

Annotated Software Bibliography *(cont.)*

JumpStart Math for First Graders
by Knowledge Adventure, Inc.

Frankie the Dog takes children on a math adventure through a large backyard. Many skills are featured, including counting money, telling time, weights and measures, and geometry. Appropriate for ages 5–7. Available for Windows and Macintosh.

Land Before Time Math Adventure
by Sound Source Interactive

Based on the popular movie, this interactive program helps children ages 4–8 to learn numbers, problem solving, estimation, and greater than/less than. Available for Windows or Macintosh.

Math Blaster 4–6
by Knowledge Adventure

Join Blasternaut and friends for energetic practice with addition, subtraction, colors, counting, estimation, patterns, and shapes. Ten space activities with three levels of difficulty make this program a "blast" for kids. Available for Windows and Macintosh.

Millie's Math House
by Edmark

In this game, children play seven fun games in the house of Millie, the cow. Math skills include counting, numbers, addition, subtraction, patterning, and problem solving. Appropriate for ages 2–5. Available for Windows and Macintosh.

Peter Rabbit's Math Garden
by Educational Insights

Math practice is fun and games with this playland filled with characters based on Beatrix Potter's classic tale. Your children will learn basic math skills by playing four games with increasing levels of difficulty. Appropriate for ages 4–7. Available for Windows and Macintosh.

Piggy in Numberland
by Legacy Interactive

Children journey to enchanted castles, hidden playgrounds, and secret houses where they learn numbers, counting, addition, subtraction, counting money, patterns, spatial relationships, and shapes. Appropriate for ages 4–7. Available for Windows only.

Reader Rabbit's Math: Ages 4–6
by The Learning Company

Children use numbers and solve number puzzles to win prizes with this delightful program. Children can play fifteen different games with multiple levels of increasing difficulty. Skills include patterning, number equations, matching, measurement, and more. Available for Windows and Macintosh.

Sesame Street Numbers
by Children's Television Workshop

This program provides eight activities for learning numbers and number concepts. Activities include games, Sesame Street songs, and storybooks. Featured skills include counting, addition, subtraction, near/far, and classification. Appropriate for ages 3–6. Available for Windows and Macintosh.

Annotated Book Bibliography

Anno's Magic Seeds by Mitsumasa Anno (Philomel Books, 1995)

This game-like story poses simple mathematical questions throughout.

Bat Jamboree by Kathi Appelt (Morrow Junior Books, 1996)

This is the lively story of the annual bat jamboree, where one bat sings, two bats flap, three bats cha-cha-cha, four bats tap, and a whole lot more.

Count-A-Saurus by Nancy Blumenthal (Four Winds Press, 1989)

Your children will be delighted to see the amusing actions of ten sets of dinosaurs. This book also provides interesting information about dinosaurs.

Counting Cows by Woody Jackson (Harcourt Brace, 1995)

Children can count backwards from ten to zero in this beautifully illustrated story about cows grazing in the Vermont countryside.

Counting Crocodiles by Judy Sierra (Harcourt Brace, 1997)

A monkey counts crocodiles from one to ten in this cheerfully illustrated book.

Count on Clifford by Norman Bridwell (Scholastic Trade, 1988)

Children will enjoy this book as Clifford teaches counting skills at a birthday party.

Five Little Ducks by Raffi (Crown, 1999)

One of the Raffi *Songs to Read* series, this book helps children count little ducks backwards from five to zero.

Five Little Monkeys Jumping on the Bed by Eileen Christelow (Clarion Books, 1989)

Five energetic monkeys are up to no good as their mother calls the doctor for advice. Your children are sure to enjoy this up-beat counting book.

How Many Bugs in a Box? by David A. Carter (Little Simon, 1988)

This pop-up book teaches children to count as they determine how many bugs are in each of ten boxes.

How Many Snails? by Paul Giganti, Jr. (Greenwillow Books, 1988)

This story encourages counting skills as a young child takes a walk and wonders at the mathematical possibilities all around.

Icky Bug Counting Book by Jerry Pallotta
(Charlesbridge Publishing, 1992)

In this book, your children can learn about 26 different kinds of insects that are not so icky.

The Jacket I Wear in the Snow by Shirley Neitzel
(Mulberry Books, 1994)

It takes layers of clothes to stay warm in the snow. This story is a parody of "The House that Jack Built" and shows the frustration a child experiences while donning and shedding winter clothes.

Annotated Book Bibliography *(cont.)*

More Than One by Miriam Schlein (Greenwillow, 1996)

This book is all about the number one. The concept of one becomes more difficult as it is used to represent one pair and one week and one dozen.

One Gorilla: A Counting Book by Atsuko Morozumi (Farrar Straus & Giroux, 1990)

One gorilla counts ten different animals hidden within the illustrations in this counting book.

One Hungry Monster by Susan Heyboer O'Keefe (Little, Brown and Company, 1989)

A boy interacts with ten lively monsters in this engaging story. Children will enjoy the rhyming text as they put their counting skills to work.

The Right Number of Elephants by Jeff Sheppard (Harper & Row, Publishers, 1990)

Counting from one to ten has never been such fun. This book depicts elephants in a variety of situations that will bring giggles and smiles to your children.

Roll Over! A Counting Song by Merle Peck (Clarion Books, 1991)

This familiar counting song helps children count backwards as t n little animals fall out of bed one by one.

Ten, Nine, Eight by Molly Bang (Demco Media, 1991)

This story is a counting lullaby. A father sings a coun' ng song from ten to one as his daughter prepares to fall asleep.